WALRUS

Sandie Lee Books

Walrus

The walrus is a large mammal that belongs to the, Odobenidae family. Its name in Latin means, "tooth-walking sea-horse." The walrus has been around for a long time. In fact, a walrus fossil was found in the San Francisco Bay. It is estimated to be about 28,000 years old. The walrus has lots of other interesting and fascinating facts to go along with it, as well. Let's explore the world of the walrus to discover more about this weird mammal.

Where in the World?

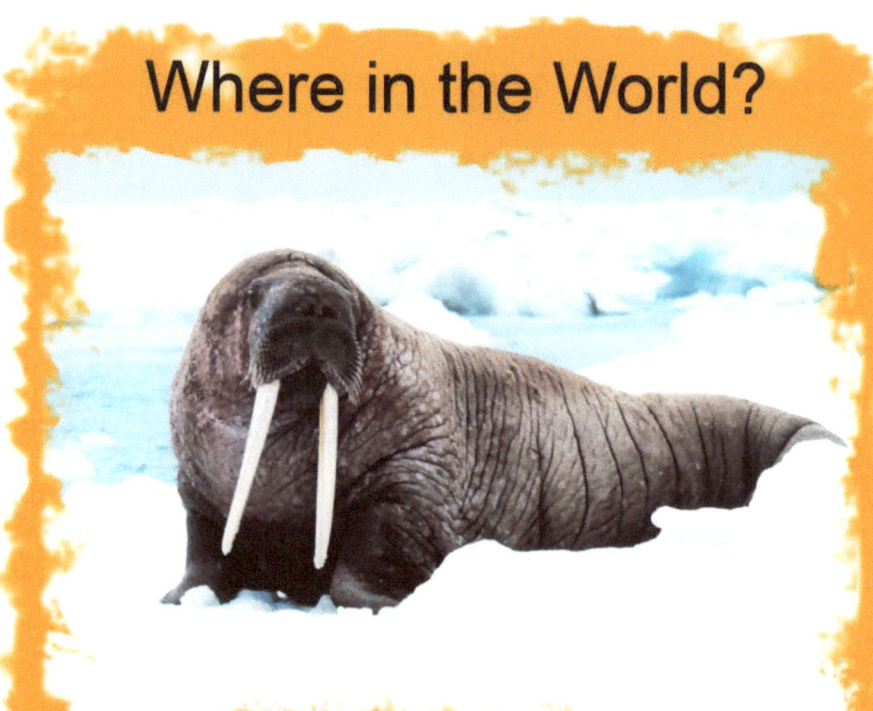

Did you know the walrus loves cold climates? This animal can be found around the North Pole, the Arctic ocean and both the North Atlantic and North Pacific oceans. It lives most of its life in the shallow waters and on ice flows. During the breeding season it will come ashore and lounge around in a large group.

The Body of a Walrus

Did you know the walrus has a very small head? The body of a walrus is roundish and is built more for moving in the water than on land. It has 2 large flippers on its front and 2 smaller flippers on its hind end. The walrus's ears are inside its tiny head. It has small wide-set eyes.

The Size of the Walrus

Did you know the walrus is bulky and huge? Some walrus can exceed weights of 4,000 pounds! The skin of the walrus is very thick - up to 6 inches. This tough skin and a thick layer of fat called, blubber, helps keep this animal warm in the frosty weather.

Walrus Tusks

Did you know the tusks of a walrus are made from ivory? Both the male and female walrus have tusks. These continue to grow throughout the walrus's lifetime. The male's tusks will be longer and wider. These tusks are considered very valuable. Man has poached this animal for the ivory in its tusks.

The Job the Tusks

Did you know the walrus uses its tusks to do many things? The tusks of the walrus help to pull this animal along on shore. The tusks are used to dig through the bottom of the ocean to find food and to also crack open the shells. Males use their long sharp tusks to show dominance and to attract a mate.

What a Walrus Eats

Did you know the walrus may only eat every few days? The walrus hunts for clams, mussels, cockles and other shellfish that live on the bottom of the ocean. The walrus can dive down 300 feet in search of food. One walrus can eat around 4,000 clams in one day.

Walrus Whiskers

Did you know the whiskers on a walrus are very sensitive? The whiskers on a walrus are called, vibrissae. These 6 inch whiskers cover the walrus's entire snout. When hunting for food under water, the vibrissae of the walrus can feel where the food is. These whiskers are constantly being worn down.

The Social Walrus

Did you know the walrus is very social? This big animal loves to be with other walruses. They will group together on large ice floes or on land. A herd of walrus can contain as many as 1,000 individuals. They will even pile on top of each other. This group is made up of males, females and their young.

The Walrus as Prey

Did you know the walrus only has 3 predators? Polar bears hunt the walrus on land and will take the young and weaker members of a herd. Orca (Killer Whales) hunt the walrus in the ocean. The third predator is man. Humans hunt this animal for its meat, blubber and tusks.

Walrus Talk

Did you know the walrus can make sounds? The walrus can make a range of noises from grunts, whistles, growls and bellows - it kind of sounds like Chewbacca from Star Wars. Most of the sound the walrus makes is done in the breeding season to attract a mate or when it feels threatened.

The Walrus Mom

Did you know the female walrus may not have a baby until she is 10 years-old? The walrus reproduce very slowly. Mom walrus (or cow) will carry her calf for 15 to 16 months. She will give birth to just one calf between the months of April and June. She nurses the baby walrus in the water.

The Baby Walrus

Did you know the baby walrus is born huge? A walrus calf can weigh as much as 165 pounds when it is first born! The calf is born already knowing how to swim. In the herd, a mother walrus will keep her calf safe under her two front flippers. The calf will stay with its mother for about 2 years.

Life of a Walrus

Did you know the walrus can live a very long time? A healthy walrus can live to be 40 years old. Some walrus have been put into special exhibits and zoos. These walrus can be trained and are very entertaining. Mostly the walrus will spend its life, eating sleeping and swimming.

Pacific Walrus

Although there is only species of walrus, the Pacific walrus is the biggest of the subspecies. This giant can exceed weights of 4,000 pounds. It spends over half of its life in the cold waters of the Arctic. There are about 200,000 of the Pacific walrus in the world today.

Quiz

Question 1: What does the walrus's name mean in Latin?

Answer 1: *Tooth-walking sea-horse*

Question 2: The walrus spends most of its time on ice flows and in the sea. When does it come to shore?

Answer 2: During the breeding season

Question 3: What expensive product are the walrus's tusks made from?

Answer 3: Ivory

Question 4: How many clams can the average walrus eat in one day?

Answer 4: 4,000

Question 5: What large land animal preys on the walrus?

Answer 5: The Polar bear

Thank you for checking out another addition from Sandie Lee Books! Make sure to check out Amazon.com for many other great titles.

www.ingramcontent.com/pod-product-compliance
Lightning Source LLC
Chambersburg PA
CBHW050803290526
45792CB00008B/2301